Veg Slow Cooker Cookbook

Easy and Healthy Vegan Crock Pot Recipes

Sarah Spencer

ISBN: 978-1984984456

Printed in the United States

COOK BOOK
THE
PUBLISHER

Contents

Introduction

A vegan diet contains foods of a vegetable nature only. Following this diet, you'll consume grains, nuts, fruits, beans, legumes, and of course, vegetables. Like vegetarianism, it can be a very healthy way to eat. Veganism does differ from vegetarianism, though, in both the foods allowed in the diet, and the reasons behind it.

Vegetarians don't eat meat, either because they don't like it, for health reasons, or because they protest the consumption of animals. Vegans don't eat meat, either – or *any* food from animals, including dairy and eggs. In fact, vegans often don't like to be lumped in with vegetarians, because their motivations are ethical in nature.

Vegans are opposed to the slaughter of animals, certainly. But they also recognize that there is killing involved in the dairy industry as well (male calves are often taken at birth, and either culled or sold for veal). Additionally, animals raised as food are often subject to poor (many would say cruel) living conditions. Vegans oppose these practices.

Additionally, vegans often realize that their way of eating is better for the environment. There is a lot of deforestation taking place to make room for farming, much of it soy, most of which goes to feed the animals we eat. Massive quantities of grain go to these animals, while in other countries, people are starving. So there are human rights aspects to this lifestyle, as well.

Naturally, vegans don't use other animal products either (like leather, for instance), and they oppose animal testing for any reason.

Many of these concerns have never occurred to the average consumer, and on their own they are compelling. However, there are advantages for your body, as well.

1. **A vegan diet is richer in certain nutrients.** Whole-food vegan diets are generally higher in certain nutrients. However, you do need to make sure you get all the nutrients your body needs. It's advisable to speak with a doctor or nutritionist, to make sure you know how to replace the proteins you'll be eliminating.

2. **A vegan diet can help you lose excess weight.** Vegan diets have a natural tendency to reduce your calorie intake. This makes them effective at promoting weight loss without the need to actively focus on cutting calories.

3. **Veganism appears to lower blood sugar levels and improve kidney function.** Vegan diets may reduce the risk of developing type 2 diabetes. They are also particularly effective at reducing blood sugar levels and may help prevent further health problems from developing.

4. **Veganism is linked to a lower risk of heart disease.** Vegan diets may benefit heart health by significantly reducing the risk factors that contribute to heart disease, such as saturated fat.

5. **A vegan diet can reduce pain from arthritis.** Vegan diets based on probiotic-rich whole foods can significantly decrease the symptoms of osteoarthritis and rheumatoid arthritis, because vegan foods would tend to discourage the inflammation that causes the pain.

If you're following a vegan lifestyle, you may know these things already. In that case, you're probably also familiar with the amount of work that goes into eating so carefully. That brings us to the topic of slow cookers.

The Benefits of Using a Slow Cooker

1. **Slow cookers can be very convenient.** Slow cookers are not just for cooking meat. Vegans work and have families, too – and wouldn't you like to come home to a meal that is all ready to go?

2. **Slow cookers save energy.** Slow cookers consume much less energy than an electric oven. Your standard oven uses about 4,000 watts per hour. On the other hand, slow cookers consume only 300 watts.

3. **The meals are super easy to make.** Anyone can master slow cooker meals, because almost all the ingredients in the recipes are added at the same time. You may need to jiggle it to distribute the liquid and spices, but that's it. Put on the lid and leave it on. The kitchen cover seals in the moisture and the flavor.

4. **Slow cookers are very safe to use.** Slow cookers are designed to be left unattended. Their maximum power is 300 watts, equivalent to the operation of three 100-watt incandescent bulbs. It is almost impossible to burn your food, and so as long as the wires aren't frayed, they're very safe. Since the ovens are well covered, there is little risk that the food will dry out and burn, which can be a problem when using the oven.

5. **Cooking at lower heat is healthier.** We recognize that vegetables are healthiest when they're raw. But if we don't want raw food all the time, steaming, poaching, and slow cooking are the healthiest ways to cook not only for food.

Breakfast Recipes

Peach Granola Crumble

A quick and easy recipe for a vegan peach crumble that you can prepare in your slow cooker. It's a healthy breakfast.

Serves 6 – Preparation time 15 minutes – Cooking time 3 hours

Ingredients
4 peaches
4 tablespoons vegan butter, melted, divided
½ cup peach juice
¼ cup agave nectar
2 cups granola, your favorite kind
2 teaspoons ground cinnamon
1 teaspoon ground nutmeg

Preparation
1. Peel and slice the peaches. In a large mixing bowl, toss them with 2 tablespoons melted vegan butter, the peach juice, and agave nectar.
2. Arrange the mixture in the bottom of a slow cooker.
3. In the same mixing bowl, stir together the granola, the remaining butter, ground cinnamon, and ground nutmeg.
4. Sprinkle the topping over the peach slices.
5. Cover the slow cooker and cook on HIGH for 3 hours. Remove the lid, turn off the slow cooker, and let the crisp cool.
6. Serve warm.

Nutrition facts per serving
Calories 232, total fat 4 g, carbs 46.5 g, protein 5.5 g,
Sodium 32.2 mg, sugar 1.1 g

Overnight Millet and Oats

This healthy millet and oats pot is very tasty! With dates and apples, this is a new twist on oatmeal.

Serves 6 – Preparation time 5 minutes – Cooking time 7 hours

Ingredients
½ cup millet
1 ½ cups steel cut oats (no substitutes)
4 ½ cups almond milk
4 tablespoons brown sugar
2 tablespoons real maple syrup
¼ teaspoon salt
1 ½ teaspoons vanilla extract
¼ cup apples, finely chopped
¼ cup dates, pitted and chopped
Optional: ¼ teaspoon ground cinnamon, fresh berries, splash of almond or soy milk, Additional sugar for topping

Preparation
1. Spray your slow cooker with non-stick spray.
2. Place the millet in a mesh sieve, and rinse well.
3. Combine the rinsed millet, steel cut oats, almond milk, brown sugar, maple syrup, salt, and vanilla extract in the slow cooker. Add the apples and dates, and any other desired toppings.
4. Stir well, and set the slow cooker on LOW.
5. Cook for 6–7 hours.
6. After 7 hours, turn off the slow cooker. Ladle it into serving dishes, and garnish with additional toppings if desired.

Nutrition facts per serving
Calories 251, total fat 3.1 g, carbs 47.7 g, protein 13.4 g, Sodium 175 mg, sugar 15.9 g

Healthy Breakfast Casserole

This is the perfect vegan breakfast to feed a crowd. Whether for a holiday or a casual Saturday, you will love this vegan, simmered breakfast that you can set up overnight.

Serves 4 – Preparation time 15 minutes – Cooking time 4 hours

Ingredients
1 cup tofu
½ cup milk
1 tablespoon ground mustard
¼ teaspoon garlic salt
½ teaspoon salt
¼ teaspoon pepper
1 (15-ounce) bag frozen hash browns
¼ onion, roughly chopped
1 bell pepper, roughly chopped
½ small head of broccoli, roughly chopped
6 ounces vegan cheddar cheese (optional)

Preparation
1. In a blender, combine the tofu and milk, and purée until smooth.
2. In a medium-sized bowl, whisk together the tofu purée, mustard, garlic salt, salt, and pepper. Set aside.
3. Lightly grease the bottom of your slow cooker. Place half the hash browns on the bottom. Layer with chopped onion, bell peppers, broccoli, and vegan cheese (if using). Add the rest of the hash browns, then top with the rest of the onion, bell peppers, broccoli, and cheese. Pour the purée mixture on top.

4. Cover the slow cooker and cook for 4 hours on LOW. After 4 hours, turn off the slow cooker, and remove the lid carefully.
5. Serve hot!

Nutrition facts per serving
Calories 220, total fat 11.2 g, carbs 19.5 g, protein 22.1 g, Sodium 735 mg, sugar 1.9 g

Chia Seed Energy Bar Recipe

Serves 4 – Preparation time 10 minutes – Cooking time 4 hours

Ingredients
1 tablespoon almond butter
1 tablespoon maple syrup
½ cup unsweetened vanilla almond milk
Pinch of salt
1 banana
¼ teaspoon cinnamon
3 tablespoons chia seed
¼ cup raisins
3 tablespoons roasted almonds, roughly chopped
3 tablespoons dried apples, roughly chopped

Preparation
1. Spray a 5-quart slow cooker with cooking spray and cut a piece of parchment to fit the bottom.
2. Mix the almond butter and maple syrup in a large bowl and microwave for about 30 seconds, until the almond butter is melted and creamy.
3. Add the almond milk and salt, and beat until the milk is well incorporated.
4. Mash the banana until well blended and add it to the almond butter mixture, together with the cinnamon, chia seed, raisins, almonds, and dried apple. Mix thoroughly.
5. Pour the mixture into the slow cooker and cook on LOW until the top of the bars is firm, about 4 hours.
6. Carefully remove the bars from the slow cooker. Put them in the refrigerator to cool completely.
7. Cut into your choice of shape, and serve. Leftovers can be stored in an airtight container, or frozen.

Nutrition facts per serving
Calories 350, total fat 10 g, carbs 70 g, protein 5 g,
Sodium 255 mg, sugar 25 g

Vegan Pumpkin Spice Syrup

Serves 4 – Preparation time 10 minutes – Cooking time 7 hours

Ingredients
2 cans full-fat coconut milk
2 cups packed light brown sugar
2 cups organic pumpkin purée
1 teaspoon ground cinnamon
1 teaspoon ground ginger
¼ teaspoon ground cardamom
¼ teaspoon ground allspice
Pinch of cloves

Preparation
1. In your slow cooker, combine the coconut milk, brown sugar, pumpkin puree , cinnamon, ground ginger, ground cardamom , ground allspice and cloves. Mix well with a whisk, and cook on LOW for 7 hours.
2. When the cooking time is up, use a whisk to thoroughly mix all the ingredients and break the pieces that are still in the syrup.
3. Keeps in the refrigerator for up to 1 week.

Nutrition facts per serving
Calories 33, total fat 0 g, carbs 7 g, protein 0 g,
Sodium 0 mg, sugar 5 g

Apple Crumble Breakfast Pudding

Serves 6 – Preparation time 10 minutes – Cooking time 4 hours

Ingredients
Pudding
1 cup almond milk
2 cups water
2 tablespoons maple syrup
½ cup chia seeds
2 tablespoons cornstarch
1 teaspoon ground cinnamon
1 pinch salt
5 large apples, sliced – do not peel!

Cinnamon Crunch Topping
½ cup blanched almond flour
¼ cup unsweetened shredded coconut
¼ cup coconut sugar
1 teaspoon cinnamon
¼ cup unsweetened apple sauce
1 teaspoon pure vanilla extract

For serving: raisins, nuts, almond milk

Preparation
1. Mix the almond milk, water, maple syrup, chia seeds, cornstarch, cinnamon, and salt in the bottom of your 3-quart crock pot.
2. Arrange the cut apples on top, and do not combine them.
3. Mix the crunch topping ingredients in a large bowl. Sprinkle them on top of the apples. Cook on LOW for 2–4 hours.

4. Turn off the slow cooker, and let it stand for an hour, uncovered.
5. Garnish with raisins, nuts, and almond milk if desired. Enjoy!

Nutrition facts per serving
Calories 363, total fat 21.5 g, carbs 49.3 g, protein 3.8 g, Sodium 157 mg, sugar 35 g

Bean and Grain Recipes

Baked Beans

Delicious homemade beans that can be served as a main course. Especially ideal for lazy Sundays or frozen for later.

Serves 4 – Preparation time 15 minutes – Cooking time 8 hours

Ingredients
1 ½ cups of dried white navy beans, soaked overnight
1 teaspoon salt
3 sundried tomatoes, cut in narrow strips
1 large onion, chopped
4 cups water
½ cup ketchup
¼ cup brown sugar, packed
2 tablespoons molasses
1 teaspoon dry mustard

Preparation
1. Drain the soaked beans, and add them to the slow cooker with the salt, sundried tomatoes, onion, and water.
2. Cover the slow cooker, and simmer on HIGH for 5–6 hours, or until tender. Add more water if the mixture begins to dry out
3. Combine the ketchup, brown sugar, molasses, and mustard in a bowl. Pour over the beans and mix.
4. Continue cooking on LOW for 1–2 hours.

Nutrition facts per serving
Calories 193, total fat 0.7 g, carbs 35.9 g, protein 7.8 g,
Sodium 84 7mg, sugar 5.9 g

Vegan Chili

All-time favorite for vegans. This recipe is loaded with sweet potatoes, bell peppers, and a variety of beans.

Serves 2 – Preparation time 20 minutes – Cooking time 8 hours

Ingredients
½ medium red onion, chopped
½ green bell pepper, chopped
2 garlic cloves, chopped
½ tablespoon chili powder
½ tablespoon ground cumin
1 teaspoon unsweetened cocoa powder
⅛ teaspoon ground cinnamon
1 teaspoon kosher salt
¼ teaspoon black pepper
½ (28-ounce) can fire roasted tomatoes, diced
½ (15.5-ounce) can black beans, rinsed
½ (15.5-ounce) can kidney beans, rinsed
1 medium sweet potato
1 cup water

For serving: sour cream, scallions, chopped cilantro, and tortilla chips

Preparation
1. In a 4- to 6-quart slow cooker, combine the onion, bell pepper, garlic, chili powder, cumin, cocoa, cinnamon, salt, and black pepper. Add the tomatoes (and their liquid), beans, sweet potato, and water.
2. Cover and cook on LOW for 7–8 hours, until the potatoes are tender and the liquid has thickened.
3. Serve with sour cream, scallions, cilantro, and tortilla chips

Nutrition facts per serving
Calories 174, total fat 2 g, carbs 35 g, protein 7 g,
Sodium 834 mg, sugar 7g

Red Beans and Rice

This is a traditional recipe that everyone loves, and it's made easy in the slow cooker!

Serves 4 – Preparation time 15 minutes – Cooking time 8 hours

Ingredients
3 cups water
8 ounces dry kidney beans
1 onion, chopped
½ green bell pepper, chopped
½ stalk celery, chopped, or to taste
2 cloves garlic, minced, or to taste
1 bay leaf
Salt and pepper to taste
Hot cooked rice, for serving

Preparation
1. Combine the water, kidney beans, onion, green bell pepper, celery, garlic, and bay leaf in the bowl of a slow cooker and stir to combine. Set the slow cooker to LOW, and cook for at least 8 hours. Remove and discard the bay leaf.
2. Meanwhile, cook the rice according to the package directions. Serve with the red bean mixture.
3. Season with salt and ground black pepper to taste.

Nutrition facts per serving
Calories 286.5, total fat 9.7 g, carbs 42 g, protein 16.5 g, Sodium 322 mg, sugar 1.7 g

Spicy Chipotle Black-Eyed Peas

Black-eyes peas are the perfect comfort food, and this healthy recipe only takes a little while to make!

Serves 6 – Preparation time 20 minutes – Cooking time 8 hours

Ingredients
1 tablespoon olive oil
½ tablespoon balsamic vinegar
½ cup red bell pepper, chopped
½ cup celery, chopped
½ cup carrot, chopped
½ cup onion, chopped
1 teaspoon garlic, minced
1 (16-ounce) package dry black-eyed peas
2 cups water
2 teaspoons vegetable bouillon base
1 teaspoon ground cumin
½ teaspoon ground black pepper

Preparation
1. Heat the olive oil and balsamic vinegar in a pan. Sauté the red pepper, celery, carrot, onion, and garlic in the hot oil until the onion is transparent, 5–8 minutes.
2. Transfer the mixture to a slow cooker. Stir in the peas, water, and vegetable base, and stir. Add the cumin and black pepper.
3. Cook in the slow cooker over LOW until the black-eyed peas are very tender and the flavors mix, about 8 hours.

Nutrition facts per serving
Calories 245, total fat 2.9 g, carbs 45.1 g, protein 12.9 g, Sodium 855 mg, sugar 4.8 g

Three-Bean Vegan Chili

This vegan chili is a perfect blend of vegetables, spices, and protein-packed beans.

Serves 4 – Preparation time 15 minutes – Cooking time 8 hours

Ingredients
2 tablespoons vegetable oil
1 onion, finely diced
1 red bell pepper, finely diced
1 green bell pepper, finely diced
1 jalapeño pepper, seeded and minced
2 cloves garlic, minced
¼ teaspoon salt
1 tablespoon chili powder
1 teaspoon ground cumin
1 teaspoon dried oregano
2 tablespoons tomato paste
½ (28-ounce) can diced tomatoes
1 ¾ cups water
½ (15.5-ounce) can black beans
½ (15.5-ounce) can kidney beans
½ (15.5-ounce) can chickpeas
Fresh cilantro leaves (optional)

Preparation
1. Coat the bowl of a 6-quart slow cooker with the oil. Add the onion, bell peppers, jalapeño, garlic, and salt, and stir to combine. Add the chili powder, cumin, oregano, tomato paste, tomatoes, and water.
2. Cover, and cook on LOW for 4 hours.

3. Drain and rinse the beans and add them to the cooker, stirring to combine. Cover and cook on LOW for another 2–4 hours.
4. Top each serving with cilantro.

Nutrition facts per serving

Calories 245, total fat 2.9 g, carbs 45.1 g, protein 12.9 g, Sodium 855 mg, sugar 4.8 g

Wild Rice Medley

This wild rice mix recipe with pine nuts is easy to prepare in a slow cooker. Grains, nuts and vegetables combine to give this dish a wonderful texture.

Serves 6 – Preparation time 20 minutes – Cooking time 5 hours

Ingredients
1 cup uncooked wild rice
⅓ cup celery, chopped
1 tablespoon olive oil
1 teaspoon fresh thyme
¼ teaspoon salt
⅛ teaspoon pepper
1 cup onion, chopped
1 cup carrots, chopped
1 ½ cups vegetable broth
3 tablespoons pine nuts
¼ cup dried cherries, chopped
Fresh parsley, chopped, if desired

Preparation
1. Spray a slow cooker with cooking spray. Combine the wild rice, chopped celery, olive oil, thyme, salt, pepper, onion, carrots, and vegetable broth in the slow cooker.
2. Cover the slow cooker and cook on LOW for 5–6 hours, or until the rice is tender and the liquid has been absorbed.
3. In the meantime, sprinkle the pine nuts in a large pan. Cook over medium heat for 5–7 minutes, stirring frequently, until the nuts are golden brown. Set them aside.
4. Just before serving, mix the cherries and the roasted pine nuts with the wild rice. Sprinkle with parsley.

Nutrition facts per serving
Calories 375, total fat 5.0 g, carbs 51.1 g, protein 34.5 g,
Sodium 714.3 mg, sugar 4.8 g

Slow Cooker Almond Quinoa Curry

This quinoa curry with almonds is one of the easiest foods to prepare. Just throw all the ingredients in the slow cooker, and let it cook.

Serves 4 – Preparation time 15 minutes – Cooking time 4 hours

Ingredients
1 cup water
½ medium sweet potato, peeled and chopped
½ large head of broccoli, cut into florets
¼ white onion, diced
½ (15-ounce) can organic chickpeas, drained and rinsed
½ (28-ounce) can diced tomatoes
1 (14.5-ounce) can almond milk
2 tablespoons quinoa
1 garlic cloves, minced
1 tablespoon freshly grated ginger
1 tablespoon freshly grated turmeric
1 teaspoon wheat-free tamari sauce
½ teaspoon miso (or additional tamari)
¼ teaspoon chili flakes

Preparation
1. Combine all the ingredients in a slow cooker. Stir until everything is fully incorporated.
2. Turn the slow cooker to HIGH and cook for 3–4 hours, until sweet potato cooks through and the curry has thickened.

Nutrition facts per serving
Calories 507, total fat 32 g, carbs 50 g, protein 13 g,
Sodium 380 mg, sugar 11 g

Barley and Bean Tacos with Avocado Chipotle Cream

Make these tacos easily in the slow cooker. Full of barley, beans, and many vegetables, the avocado cream makes them memorable.

Serves 4 – Preparation time 15 minutes – Cooking time 6 hours

Ingredients

For the filling:
½ red onion, chopped
½ cup frozen corn
½ can black beans, drained and rinsed
½ (14-ounce) can fire-roasted diced tomatoes
½ cup barley
1 cup vegetable broth
Wedge of lime
½ teaspoon cumin
¼ teaspoon smoked paprika
¼ teaspoon salt
¼ teaspoon garlic powder

For the avocado chipotle cream:
½ ripe avocado
1 tablespoon plain Greek yogurt
1 teaspoon chipotle pepper in adobo sauce, minced
Pinch of salt, or more to taste

For serving:
Flour or corn tortillas
Cilantro, chopped
Feta, crumbled

Preparation

1. <u>To make the filling</u>, combine all the filling ingredients in a slow cooker. Stir well, cover, and simmer for 5–6 hours, until most of the liquid is absorbed and the barley is tender and chewy.
2. <u>To make the avocado chipotle cream</u>, remove the avocado pit and scoop the flesh into a medium bowl. Mash it well with a fork. Add the Greek yogurt, chopped chipotle, and salt. Mix until well blended.
3. <u>To serve</u>, spoon some of the filling into a tortilla. Garnish with avocado cream, cilantro, and feta.

Nutrition facts per serving

Calories 219.8, total fat 5.8 g, carbs 34 g, protein 9.9 g, Sodium 18.8 mg, sugar 0.2 g

Salads and Sides

Slow-Cooked Mediterranean Zucchini Salad

The lively flavors of this Mediterranean zucchini salad make it an ideal companion to all dishes.

Serves 2 – Preparation time 15 minutes – Cooking time 8 hours

Ingredients
1 red onion, sliced
2 bell peppers, sliced
1 zucchini, sliced
1 (24-ounce) can whole tomatoes
1 tablespoon smoked paprika
2 teaspoons cumin
1 teaspoon salt
Fresh black pepper to taste
Juice of one lemon
Optional: falafel, to accompany

Preparation
1. Put the onion, bell peppers, zucchini, tomatoes, paprika, cumin, salt, black pepper and lemon juice in a large slow cooker, and cook on LOW for 7–8 hours.
2. After 8 hours, carefully open the lid, serve hot.
3. Falafel to go with it is also highly recommended.

Nutrition facts per serving
Calories 71.1, total fat 1.6 g, carbs 12.7 g, protein 3.5 g, Sodium 316.8 mg, sugar 0.5 g

Garlic Cauliflower Mashed Potatoes

This dish is a game changer!

Serves 6 – Preparation time 15 minutes – Cooking time 4 hours

Ingredients
½ head of cauliflower
1 ½ cups water
2 large cloves garlic, peeled
½ teaspoon salt
1 bay leaf
½ tablespoon margarine
Salt and pepper to taste

Preparation
1. Cut the cauliflower into florets and place them in the slow cooker.
2. Add the water, garlic, salt, and bay leaf.
3. Cover, and cook on HIGH for 2–3 hours.
4. Remove the cloves of garlic and the bay leaf. Drain the water.
5. Add the margarine and let it melt.
6. Use a potato masher to make a cauliflower purée.
7. Season with salt and pepper to taste.

Nutrition facts per serving
Calories 96.4, total fat 5.9 g, carbs 10.4 g, protein 3.2 g, Sodium 553.7 mg, sugar 3.3 g

German Potato Salad

Potato salad may never be the same after you make it in a slow cooker. Sun-dried tomatoes add flavor and texture to this summertime staple.

Serves 6 – Preparation time 20 minutes – Cooking time 7 hours

Ingredients
2 tablespoons olive oil
½ cup sun-dried tomato, chopped
1 cup onion, chopped
1 cup celery, chopped
1 teaspoon salt
½ teaspoon celery seed
¼ teaspoon black pepper
1 pound small red potatoes, sliced
1 cup vegetable broth
2 tablespoons sugar
1 tablespoon cornstarch
2 tablespoons cider vinegar
1 tablespoon chopped fresh parsley leaves

Preparation
1. Heat the oil in a medium skillet. Cook the sun-dried tomatoes until they begin to crisp up, and then set them aside. Add the onions and celery to the skillet, and cook until they begin to soften. Sprinkle with salt, celery seeds, and pepper.
2. Place half the potatoes in the slow cooker, and cover them with half the onion mixture. Repeat with the remaining potatoes and vegetables.
3. Pour the broth over the contents of the slow cooker.
4. Cover, and cook on LOW for 5–6 hours.

5. Remove the potatoes from the cooker with a skimmer. Mix the sugar, cornstarch, and vinegar in a small bowl, and pour the liquid in the cooker. Gently fold in the potatoes.
6. Increase the heat level to HIGH. Cover and cook for 20 to 30 minutes or until the sauce is warmed through, and the potatoes are tender. Transfer the salad to a serving bowl, and sprinkle with parsley leaves.

Nutrition facts per serving
Calories 280, total fat 5.5 g, carbs 12.7 g, protein 3.5 g, Sodium 316.8 mg, sugar 0.5 g

Farro Salad

Farro is an ancient grain that has a smooth texture and an earthy taste. This makes it an excellent base for hearty salads and side dishes.

Serves 4 – Preparation time 15 minutes – Cooking time 2 hours 10 minutes

Ingredients
1 cup uncooked faro
2 ¾ cups water
¼ cup cider vinegar
2 tablespoons canola oil
¼ teaspoon salt
¼ teaspoon ground black pepper
2 cups celery, finely chopped
1 cup parsley leaves, chopped
1 ¼ cups cherries, halved and pitted (can substitute grapes)

Preparation
1. In a slow cooker, combine the farro, water, and vinegar. Cover, and cook on HIGH for 2 hours.
2. Remove the lid and let the farro cool for at least 10 – 15 minutes.
3. In a medium bowl, combine the oil, salt, pepper, celery, and parsley. Stir in cooled farro to combine.
4. Add the cherries or grapes, stirring to combine. Serve.

Nutrition facts per serving
Calories 334, total fat 15 g, carbs 38 g, protein 13 g, Sodium 888 mg, sugar 5 g

Tofu and Black Bean Taco Salad

This simple blend of tofu, spices, garlic, and black beans makes a hearty taco filling. Pack the leftovers to put together the tacos for lunch.

Serves 4 – Preparation time 15 minutes – Cooking time 8 hours

Ingredients
1 ½ cups tofu, diced small
2 cups dried black beans
1 (18-ounce) can chili style diced tomatoes
2 tablespoons taco seasonings (like Old El Paso)
1 teaspoon cumin
1 tablespoon lime juice
1 clove garlic, minced
1 tablespoon molasses

For serving: Soft flour tortillas, lettuce, red onion, tomato, and cashew cream.

Preparation
1. Combine the tofu, beans, diced tomatoes, spices, and lime juice in the slow cooker. Cook on LOW for 6 – 8 hours, or until the beans are tender.
2. About 20–30 minutes before serving, turn the heat up to HIGH and lightly mash some of the beans and tofu, just enough to smash a few of the beans and thicken the filling. Stir in the garlic and the molasses. Replace the lid.
3. Serve with soft flour tortillas, lettuce, tomatoes, diced red onions, and your favourite taco toppings.

Nutrition facts per serving
Calories 218.9, total fat 1.3 g, carbs 28.2 g, protein 22.4 g, Sodium 700 mg, sugar 6.3 g

Thai Summer Squash Salad with Peanut-Sauce

A flavorful, easy, and healthy cold "pasta" salad recipe! Easy to make ahead and feeds a crowd.

Serves 4 – Preparation time 15 minutes – Cooking time 8 hours

Ingredients
1 small spaghetti squash
2 cups water
2 cups broccoli, steamed
1 tablespoon sesame seeds
Optional toppings: chopped peanuts, sriracha

Light Thai Peanut Sauce
1 tablespoon brown sugar
2 tablespoons sesame oil
1 tablespoon rice wine vinegar
1 tablespoon soy sauce
2 tablespoons peanut butter
1 teaspoon ginger root, peeled and grated
1 clove garlic, minced
¼ teaspoon salt
Pinch red pepper flakes
½ teaspoon sriracha (optional)

Preparation

1. Pierce your spaghetti squash with a fork.
2. Place the spaghetti squash and 2 cups of water in a slow cooker. Close the lid and cook for 8–9 hours on LOW.
3. When done, remove the spaghetti squash from the slow cooker and let it cool for 20–30 minutes. Discard the water.
4. While the squash is cooling, prepare the sauce by combining all the ingredients in a small bowl.
5. After the squash has cooled, cut it in half and scoop out the seeds and pulp.
6. With the pulp removed, use a fork to shred the insides of the squash into spaghetti-like noodles.
7. Divide the "noodles" among four serving bowls and top each with ½ cup of broccoli, 3 tablespoons of dressing, a generous pinch of sesame seeds, and peanuts if desired. Enjoy!

Nutrition facts per serving

Calories 145.9, total fat 4.3 g, carbs 26.2 g, protein 5.4 g, Sodium 108 mg, sugar 8.3 g

Stews and Chilis

Vegan Four Bean Chili

This slow cooker vegetarian chili is vegan, gluten free, SO healthy, and loaded with veggies, spices, and different kinds of beans.

Serves 4– Preparation time 20 minutes – Cooking time 6 hours

Ingredients
1 tablespoon olive oil
1 large onion, chopped
1 green bell pepper, chopped
1 zucchini, chopped
2 stalks celery, chopped
3 garlic cloves, chopped
1 (11-ounce) can condensed black bean soup (or canned black beans in juice)
1 (15-ounce) can kidney beans, drained and rinsed
1 (15-ounce) can chickpeas, drained and rinsed (may substitute lentils)
1 (16-ounce) can vegetarian baked beans
1 (14.5-ounce) can chopped tomato puree (or a 28-ounce can of crushed tomatoes)
1 (15-ounce) can whole kernel corn, drained
1 (4-ounce) can diced chilies
1 jalapeño pepper, chopped (reduce the amount for milder chili)
1 tablespoon chili powder
1 teaspoon cumin
1 tablespoon dried parsley
1 tablespoon dried oregano
1 tablespoon dried basil
1 teaspoon marjoram

Preparation

1. Heat the olive oil in a medium skillet. Sauté the onion, pepper, zucchini and celery in a pan for about 5 minutes. Add the garlic, and cook until fragrant.
2. In a slow cooker, mix the black bean soup, kidney beans, chickpeas, baked beans, tomatoes, corn, chilies, jalapeño, and the vegetable mixture.
3. Season with the chili powder, cumin, parsley, oregano, basil, and marjoram.
4. Cook for about 6 hours on LOW.
5. Serve with tortillas, vegan cornbread, rice, or French bread.

Nutrition facts per serving

Calories 263, total fat 2.3 g, carbs 51.9 g, protein 12.9 g, Sodium 240 mg, sugar 4.6

Mushroom Lentil Buckwheat Stew

These flavors combine very well to give you a healthy, earthy taste. Serve with garlic bread.

Serves 4 – Preparation time 15 minutes – Cooking time 12 hours

Ingredients

4 cups vegetable broth
1 cup sliced fresh button mushrooms
½ ounce dried shiitake mushrooms, torn into pieces
¼ cup uncooked buckwheat
¼ cup dry lentils
2 tablespoons dried onion flakes
1 teaspoon garlic, minced
1 teaspoon dried summer savory
2 bay leaves
½ teaspoon dried basil
1 teaspoon ground black pepper
Salt to taste

Preparation

1. In a slow cooker, combine all the ingredients.
2. Cover, and cook for 10–12 hours on LOW. Remove the bay leaves before serving.

Nutrition facts per serving

Calories 224, total fat 7.5 g, carbs 32.5 g, protein 5.6 g, Sodium 1240 mg, sugar 5.1

Lentil Chili

This thick and rich vegan chili is different enough to be special, but it still has a fairly popular taste to please most people. It's the perfect chili for the fall!

Serves 4 – Preparation time 10 minutes – Cooking time 8 hours

Ingredients
½ medium onion, diced
2 cloves garlic, minced
½ jalapeño, diced, seeds removed
½ red pepper, chopped
½ yellow pepper, chopped
½ large carrot, peeled and diced
1 ½ cups vegetable broth
1 (15-ounce) can tomato sauce
1 (15-ounce) can diced tomatoes
8 ounces brown lentils, rinsed
1 (15-ounce) cans small red kidney beans, rinsed and drained
2 tablespoons chili powder
½ tablespoon cumin
Salt and black pepper, to taste

Preparation
1. Place the onion, garlic, jalapeño, red pepper, yellow pepper, carrot, vegetable broth, tomato sauce, diced tomatoes, brown lentils, red beans, chili powder, cumin, and salt and black pepper in a slow cooker. Stir well to combine.
2. Cover and cook on LOW for 6 hours. Serve warm.

Nutrition facts per serving
Calories 285, total fat 2 g, carbs 50.6 g, protein 19.1 g,
Sodium 671 mg, sugar 7.4

Corn and Red Pepper Chowder

Cozy up to a bowl of this creamy potato, corn, and red pepper chowder that's ready in few hours.

Serves 4 – Preparation time 15 minutes – Cooking time 10 hours

Ingredients

1 tablespoon olive oil
½ medium yellow onion, diced
½ medium red bell pepper, seeded and diced
2 medium red-skinned potatoes, diced
2 cups frozen sweet corn kernels, divided
2 cups vegetable broth
½ teaspoon ground cumin
¼ teaspoon smoked paprika
Pinch cayenne pepper
½ teaspoon kosher salt
½ cup coconut milk
 Salt and black pepper to taste
 To garnish: chopped red bell pepper, corn kernels, and sliced scallions

Preparation

1. Heat the olive oil in a medium-sized pan over medium heat. Add the onion and cook, stirring occasionally, until light and smooth, about 5 minutes. Transfer the onion, along with the red pepper, potatoes, 1 cup of corn, broth, cumin, smoked paprika, cayenne pepper, and salt to the slow cooker.
2. Cook on LOW for 8–10 hours, until the potatoes are tender.

3. Turn off the slow cooker and remove the lid. Let the soup cool down a bit. Blend the soup with a hand blender or a standard blender. Put it back in the pot and turn it back on.
4. Add the remaining 1 cup of corn, and the coconut milk. Cover, and heat on HIGH for 20–30 minutes, until it is warmed through. Season with salt and pepper.
5. Serve with additional corn, peppers and/or sliced green onions.

Nutrition facts per serving
Calories 85, total fat 2.2 g, carbs 16.2 g, protein 2.6 g, Sodium 163 mg, sugar 3.4

Black Bean and Quinoa Crock-Pot Stew

It's hearty, easy to make, and tastes amazing. This stew is vegan and gluten free.

Serves 4 – Preparation time 10 minutes – Cooking time 10 hours

Ingredients
1 dried chipotle pepper
8 ounces dried organic black beans, rinsed and cleaned
¼ cup uncooked quinoa, rinsed and cleaned
½ (28-ounce) can organic diced tomatoes
½ red onion, diced
2 cloves garlic, minced
½ green bell pepper, chopped
½ red bell pepper, chopped
½ dried cinnamon stick
1 teaspoon chili powder
½ teaspoon ground coriander
2 tablespoons fresh cilantro, chopped
3 ½ cups water
Salt and pepper to taste

Toppings
Cilantro
Green onions, thinly sliced
Lime wedges
Avocado
Tortilla chips

Preparation

1. Combine all the ingredients EXCEPT the salt in the slow cooker, and stir.
2. Cook on HIGH for 4–6 hours, or on LOW for 8–10 hours, until the black beans are tender.
3. Taste the mixture, and add salt as needed. Remove the chipotle pepper before serving.
4. Serve topped with fresh cilantro, green onions, a squeeze of fresh lime juice, diced avocados, tortilla chips, etc.

Nutrition facts per serving

Calories 310, total fat 2.5 g, carbs 576 g, protein 17 g, Sodium 150 mg, sugar 5.4

Lentil Cauliflower Stew

An easy slow cooker recipe for cauliflower stew with lentils for a healthful, stick-to-your-ribs meal.

Serves 6 – Preparation time 30 minutes – Cooking time 8 hours

Ingredients
1 tablespoon olive oil
2 onions, chopped
2 cloves garlic, chopped
16 ounces dried lentils
1 large head cauliflower, chopped into very small florets
2 leeks (white and green parts only) halved, washed carefully, and chopped
2 large carrots, peeled and chopped
3 celery ribs, chopped
2 bay leaves
1 tablespoon fresh thyme or 1 teaspoon dried thyme
2 tablespoons kosher salt (or to taste)
1 teaspoon cumin
½ teaspoon cayenne
¼ teaspoon black pepper
8 cups low sodium vegetable broth
32 ounces canned tomatoes with juice, diced
2 cups kale, chopped

For topping, optional: cashew cream, chopped coriander or parsley, green onion

Preparation

1. Heat the oil in a saucepan over medium heat. Cook the onions for about 4 minutes, until soft. Add the chopped garlic and sauté for another minute.
2. Pour the onions and garlic into the slow cooker, and add the remaining ingredients.
3. Cover the slow cooker and cook on HIGH for 6 hours, or for 8 hours on LOW.
4. Remove the bay leaves before serving.
5. Serve hot with your choice of toppings.

Nutrition facts per serving

Calories 160, total fat 6 g, carbs 19 g, protein 7 g, Sodium 690 mg, sugar 10 g

Root Vegetable and Tempeh Vegan Chili

This chili recipe packs a powerful protein boost and has a satisfying texture. It's also gluten free.

Serves 6 – Preparation time 10 minutes – Cooking time 6 hours

Ingredients
1 cup rutabaga, peeled and cubed
1 cup turnip, peeled and cubed
1 cup sweet potato, peeled and cubed
1 cup parsnip, peeled and cubed
½ cup carrots, peeled and cubed
½ cup beets, peeled and cubed
½ cup yellow onion, diced
4 ounces gluten-free tempeh, rinsed and cubed
½ cup vegetable broth
½ (28-ounce) can diced tomatoes
½ (15-ounce) can kidney beans, rinsed
½ (15-ounce) can black beans, rinsed
½ teaspoon kosher sea salt, divided
½ teaspoon cayenne pepper, divided
½ teaspoon chili powder, divided
½ teaspoon ground cumin, divided
¼ teaspoon paprika, divided
¼ teaspoon nutmeg, divided

Toppings:
½ cup vegan sour cream, for garnish
½ cup vegan cheese shreds, for garnish
¼ cup flat leaf parsley, chopped, for garnish

Preparation

1. Peel and cut the vegetables into ½-inch cubes, keeping all the pieces the same size so they cook evenly. Mix the vegetables together in a 6-quart slow cooker.
2. Rinse and cut the tempeh into ½-inch cubes, then layer it over the vegetables.
3. Pour the vegetable stock and the diced tomatoes over the tempeh, and add the kidney and black beans.
4. Cover the slow cooker and set it on LOW. After 2 hours, add the spices and stir to combine all the ingredients. Put the lid back on and cook for another 4 hours.
5. After a total of six hours, check the stew. If the vegetables and the tempeh are soft, turn off the slow cooker and serve the chili. Otherwise, cook for another hour on LOW.
6. Serve the chili in large bowls with toppings.

Nutrition facts per serving

Calories 260, total fat 7.1 g, carbs 35.8 g, protein 17.3 g, Sodium 822.2 mg, sugar 8.1g

Vegetable Recipes

Balsamic Pear, Mushroom, and Asparagus

An unusual blend of spices enlivens this slow-cooked dish, which benefits from the abundance of asparagus in the spring. In other seasons, fresh green beans would be a good option to replace asparagus.

Serves 4 – Preparation time 10 minutes – Cooking time 6 hours

Ingredients
1 tablespoon vegetable oil
2 pounds mushrooms, sliced
1 onion, sliced
2 ripe Bartlett pears, cored and sliced
1 pound fresh asparagus, trimmed
4 cloves garlic, minced
2 tablespoons balsamic vinegar
3 tablespoons apple juice
1 teaspoon dried rosemary
1 tablespoon fresh ginger, grated
2 tablespoons dark brown sugar
Salt and pepper

Preparation
1. Heat the oil in a saucepan over medium heat. Cook the mushrooms in the hot oil until golden, 3–5 minutes. Transfer them to a slow cooker.
2. Add the onion to the mushrooms, and season with salt and pepper. Add the pears and asparagus.

3. In a medium-sized bowl, combine the garlic, balsamic vinegar, apple juice, rosemary, ginger, and sugar in a bowl; pour it over the asparagus. Season with salt and pepper.
4. Cook over LOW for 4 to 6 hours.

Nutrition facts per serving
Calories 255, total fat 3 g, carbs 27.8 g, protein 27.6 g, Sodium 214.2 mg, sugar 8.1g

Baked Sweet Potatoes

Cooking sweet potatoes in the slow cooker makes them extra moist and sweet!

Serves 4– Preparation time 10 minutes – Cooking time 8 hours

Ingredients
4 medium sweet potatoes, washed and dried
4 sheets of aluminum foil

Preparation
1. Poke the sweet potatoes 3–4 times with a fork.
2. Wrap each sweet potato in aluminum foil and place them in the slow cooker, and cover. You do not need any liquid in the slow cooker.
3. Cook on LOW for 8 hours, or until tender.

Nutrition facts per serving
Calories 316, total fat 3.4 g, carbs 29.3 g, protein 41.2 g, Sodium 1561.3 mg, sugar 3.1 g

Rosemary and Red Pepper Tofu

Lunch won't be dull with this tasty, make-ahead meal.

Serves 4 – Preparation time 20 minutes – Cooking time 6 hours

Ingredients
1 small onion, thinly sliced
1 medium red bell pepper, seeded and thinly sliced
4 cloves garlic, minced
2 teaspoons dried rosemary
½ teaspoon dried oregano
8s tofu
¼ teaspoon coarsely ground pepper
¼ cup dry vermouth
1 ½ tablespoons cornstarch
2 tablespoons cold water
Salt to taste
¼ cup chopped fresh parsley

Preparation
1. In a 6-quart slow cooker, combine the onion, bell pepper, garlic, rosemary, and oregano. Add the tofu, and arrange it in a single layer over the onion. Sprinkle with pepper. Pour in the vermouth. Cover, and cook on LOW for 5–7 hours.
2. Transfer tofu to a warm, deep platter, and cover to keep warm.
3. In a small bowl, stir together the cornstarch and cold water. Stir it into the cooking liquid in the slow cooker. Increase the heat to HIGH, and cover. Cook, stirring a few times, until sauce is thickened (about 10 more minutes).
4. Season to taste with salt. Spoon the sauce over the tofu, and sprinkle with parsley.

Nutrition facts per serving
Calories 165, total fat 1.6 g, carbs 3.5 g, protein 27.8 g,
Sodium 226.3 mg, sugar 0.9 g

Enchilada Amaranth

This easy slow cooker recipe is a family favorite! Serve tortilla chips or tortillas on the side!

Serves 4 – Preparation time 15 minutes – Cooking time 6 hours

Ingredients
1 cup uncooked amaranth, rinsed
½ cup water
1 small onion, diced
2 cloves garlic, minced
1 red pepper, seeds removed, diced
2 (15-ounce) cans black beans, rinsed and drained
2 (10-ounce) cans red enchilada sauce
1 (15-ounce) can diced tomatoes
1 (4.5-ounce) can chopped green chilies
1 cup corn frozen kernels
Juice of 1 small lime
1 teaspoon ground cumin
1 tablespoon chili powder
⅓ cup chopped cilantro
Salt and black pepper, to taste
1 ½ cups shredded vegan cheese

Optional toppings: Sliced green onions, avocado, diced tomatoes, cashew cream, cilantro, and lime wedges

Preparation

1. Mix the all the ingredients EXCEPT the cheese in a 6-quart slow cooker. Mix to combine. Season with salt and pepper. Cover, and cook on HIGH for 3 hours, or on LOW 6 hours, until the amaranth is cooked.
2. Remove the lid and mix the casserole. Test and adjust the spice if necessary. Stir in half the cheese, and sprinkle the other half on top. Replace the lid, and cook until the cheese has melted, about 15 minutes.
3. Serve hot with the desired toppings.

Nutrition facts per serving

Calories 270, total fat 9.7 g, carbs 38.1 g, protein 11.6 g, Sodium 468.3 mg, sugar 4.5 g

Quick and Easy Swiss Cauliflower

Need healthy slow cooker recipes? We've got you covered! This veggie-filled side dish will go great with just about any meal.

Serves 6– Preparation time 25 minutes – Cooking time 6 hours

Ingredients
2 cups broccoli florets
2 cups cauliflower florets
½ (14-ounce) jar vegan alfredo pasta sauce
3 ounces vegan Swiss cheese, sliced
½ large onion, chopped
½ teaspoon dried thyme, oregano, or basil, crushed
⅛ teaspoon ground black pepper
¼ cup sliced almonds

Preparation
1. In a 4-quart slow cooker, combine the broccoli, cauliflower, pasta sauce, vegan cheese, onion, thyme, and pepper.
2. Cover, and cook on LOW for 6–7 hours, or on HIGH for 3 hours.
3. Stir gently before serving. If desired, sprinkle with almonds.

Nutrition facts per serving
Calories 177, total fat 12 g, carbs 10 g, protein 27.8 g, Sodium 573 mg sugar 4g

Tempeh with Apples, Sweet Potatoes, and Sauerkraut

In this lovely side, sweet potatoes are slow-cooked with apples and spices. It's perfect for any special occasion.

Serves 4 – Preparation time 15 minutes – Cooking time 5hours

Ingredients
2 large apples, peeled, cored, and cut into bite-sized pieces
4 medium sweet potatoes, peeled and cut into 1 ½-inch pieces
1 ½ cups apple juice or ¾ cup apple cider
20 ounces tempeh
4 cups wine-cured sauerkraut
1 teaspoon caraway seed (optional)
⅔ cup honey mustard

Preparation
1. Arrange the apple and sweet potato in the bottom of the slow cooker. Pour in the apple juice.
2. Add the tempeh, and cover it with the sauerkraut. Sprinkle in the caraway seed.
3. Smear the mustard on top.
4. Cover, and cook on LOW for 5 hours.

Nutrition facts per serving
Calories 120, total fat 2.9 g, carbs 24.7 g, protein 0.8 g, Sodium 15.3 mg, sugar 4 g

Vegetable Red Curry

This is a satisfying and comforting vegan dish packed with protein and full of flavor, thanks to the warm spices.

Serves 6 – Preparation time 15 minutes – Cooking time 7 hours

Ingredients
4 tablespoons red curry paste
2 cups full fat coconut milk
1 tablespoon creamy peanut butter
4 cups vegetable broth
2 tablespoons maple syrup
8 scallions, chopped
2 red bell peppers, sliced into strips
2 green bell peppers, sliced into strips
4 cups chickpeas
2 cups carrots, sliced
2 tablespoons ginger, freshly minced
2 tablespoons soy sauce
2 Thai chilies, thinly sliced
2 tablespoons fresh lime juice
1 cup rice
⅓ cup Thai basil

Preparation
1. Stir the red curry paste with the coconut milk and peanut butter until smooth. Spoon the mixture into the slow cooker, and add the broth, maple syrup, scallions, red bell pepper, green bell pepper, chickpeas, carrots, ginger, soy sauce, Thai chilies, and lime juice.
2. Cover, and cook on LOW for 6 hours.
3. Add the rice. Increase the heat to HIGH and cook for 30–45 minutes, depending on the type of rice.
4. Add the Thai basil, and serve immediately.

Nutrition facts per serving
Calories 164, total fat 7.6 g, carbs 17.3 g, protein 7.2 g,
Sodium 449.6 mg, sugar 3.3 g

Mediterranean Stuffed Peppers

Hearty peppers loaded with protein and fiber, and packed with so much flavor, all made in the slow cooker.

Serves 2 – Preparation time 15 minutes – Cooking time 4 hours

Ingredients
2 large bell peppers
½ (15-ounce) can cannellini beans, rinsed and drained
¼ cup couscous, cooked
2 scallions, white and green parts separated, thinly sliced
1 clove garlic, minced
½ teaspoon dried oregano
Coarse salt and freshly ground pepper
Lemon wedges, for serving

Preparation
1. Cut a very thin layer off the base of each pepper so they sit flat. Slice the top, straight across under the stem, to make a cup. Discard the stems. Remove the ribs and seeds from the peppers.
2. Add the beans, couscous, scallions (the white parts), garlic, and oregano to the bowl. Season with salt and pepper, and mix. Fill the peppers with the bean mixture, and place them in the slow cooker in a vertical position. Cover, and cook on HIGH for 4 hours.
3. Sprinkle the peppers with the scallion greens, and serve with lemon slices.

Nutrition facts per serving
Calories 380, total fat 22.3 g, carbs 27.3 g, protein 17.2 g, Sodium 222 mg, sugar 1.3 g

Eggplant Lasagna

Healthy, gluten free, and your slow cooker does all the work! Slow cooker Low Carb Lasagna is made with eggplant in place of pasta.

Serves 6 – Preparation time 20 minutes – Cooking time 4 hours

Ingredients

1 medium eggplant (1 pound), cut into ¼-inch thick rounds
2 teaspoons salt
1 container soft (silken) tofu
1 container firm or extra firm tofu
¼ cup soy milk
2 cups vegan ricotta
2 tablespoons chopped fresh basil
2 cloves garlic, minced
1 teaspoon Italian seasoning
3 ½ cups marinara sauce, warmed
1 cup vegan cheese blend

Preparation

1. Arrange the eggplant in a single layer on 2 racks. Sprinkle with 1 teaspoon salt. Let stand for 10 minutes. Turn the slices and repeat the process. Rinse off the salt, and dry the slices between clean kitchen towels.
2. In a food processor or blender, combine the silken tofu, the firm or extra-firm tofu, and the soy milk.
3. Combine the vegan ricotta with the tofu mixture, and add the basil, garlic, and Italian seasoning in a bowl.
4. Coat a slow cooker with cooking spray. Add ¾ cup warm marinara sauce. Top with eggplant slices, overlapping to fit. Spread half of the ricotta mixture over the eggplant. Layer on more eggplant slices, and then 1 cup of the

marinara sauce and ¼ cup shredded vegan cheese. Repeat with another layer of eggplant, remaining ricotta mixture, remaining eggplant, 1 cup marinara sauce and ¼ cup shredded cheese. Finish with the last of the marinara, reserving ½ cup of the shredded cheese for later.

5. Cover, and cook 4–5 hours on low. Sprinkle the remaining ½ cup vegan cheese over the top. Cover, and let it stand until the cheese melts. Uncover, and cool for 20 minutes.
6. Serve and enjoy!

Nutrition facts per serving
Calories 420, total fat 18.9 g, carbs 37.1 g, protein 36.1 g, Sodium 1500 mg, sugar 8.2 g

Summer Vegetable Succotash Recipe

The word *succotash* comes from a Narragansett word, which means cooked corn. The dish is a soothing combination of corn, beans, and other local, seasonal vegetables.

Serves 4 – Preparation time 15 minutes – Cooking time 4 hours

Ingredients
½ (10-ounce) can seasoned diced tomatoes in juice
¼ cup vegetable broth
1 cup corn kernels
1 cup diced zucchini
½ cup sliced okra
3 tablespoons white onion, minced
2 cloves garlic, minced
¼ teaspoon salt
⅛ teaspoon ground black pepper
⅛ teaspoon red pepper flakes
1 tablespoon lemon juice
¼ teaspoon hot sauce
¼ teaspoon dried parsley

Preparation
1. Put the slow cooker on LOW. Add the tomatoes with their juice, and the vegetable broth.
2. Add the corn, zucchini, okra, onion, and garlic. Sprinkle with the salt, pepper, and red pepper flakes. Mix to combine.
3. Cover, and cook for 4 hours on LOW.
4. Before serving the succotash, mix the lemon juice and the hot sauce. Add the parsley and mix.
5. Spoon the mixture over the succotash, and stir to combine.

Nutrition facts per serving
Calories 206, total fat 10.8 g, carbs 27.3 g, protein 4.4 g,
Sodium 197.2 mg, sugar 9.4 g

Soups and Bowls

Yellow Pea Soup

Something magical happens when the split peas break down into a thick soup, naturally creamy and delicious after several hours in the slow cooker.

Serves 4 – Preparation time 10 minutes – Cooking time 8 hours

Ingredients
1 pound yellow split peas, rinsed and sorted
1 cup carrots, julienned
½ teaspoon dried thyme leaves
½ teaspoon dried marjoram leaves
¼ teaspoon pepper
2 cups vegetable broth
1 ½ cups water

Preparation
1. In 3- to 4-quart slow cooker, mix the yellow split peas, carrots, thyme, marjoram, pepper, vegetable broth, and water.
2. Cover, and cook on LOW for 8–10 hours.
3. Increase the heat setting to HIGH, and stir well. Cover and cook 30 minutes longer.

Nutrition facts per serving
Calories 198, total fat 4.7 g, carbs 21.3g, protein 18.2 g, Sodium 1466.5 mg, sugar 3.6 g

Lentil Tortilla Soup

This easy and crazy flavorful soup can be made in a pressure cooker or a slow cooker.

Serves 4 – Preparation time 10 minutes – Cooking time 6 hours

Ingredients

1 cup onion, diced
1 teaspoon avocado oil or olive oil
1 bell pepper, diced
1 jalapeño pepper, diced
2 ½ cups vegetable broth
1 (15-ounce) can tomato sauce or crushed tomatoes, extra to taste
½ cup salsa verde (or your favorite salsa!)
1 tablespoon tomato paste
1 (15-ounce) can black beans, drained and rinsed
1 (15-ounce) can pinto beans, drained and rinsed
1 cup corn (fresh, canned, or frozen)
¾ cup dried red lentils
½ teaspoon chili powder
½ teaspoon garlic powder
½ teaspoon cumin
¼ teaspoon cayenne pepper
¼-½ cup cashew cream
Salt and pepper to taste
Toppings of your choice

Preparation

1. In a 6-quart slow cooker, combine all the ingredients EXCEPT the cream and toppings. Cook on HIGH for 5–6 hours, until the lentils are cooked through and the veggies are tender.
2. Swirl in the cashew cream, add all your favourite toppings, and serve.

Nutrition facts per serving

Calories 188, total fat 5.6g, carbs 25 g, protein 11.6 g,
Sodium 369.5 mg, sugar 4.4 g

Lemon Rosemary Lentil Soup

Fresh vegetables, lemon, and rosemary become an amazingly hearty soup with minimal effort.

Serves 4 – Preparation time 15 minutes – Cooking time 6 hours

Ingredients
3 carrots, peeled and diced
½ large onion, diced
2 cloves garlic, minced
½ yellow pepper, chopped
Pinch cayenne pepper
1 ½ cups red lentils
2 cups vegetable broth
1 ½ cups water
1 teaspoon salt
½ teaspoon lemon zest
Juice of half a lemon
½ tablespoon fresh rosemary, chopped, plus some for garnish

Preparation
1. In a 6-quart slow cooker, combine the carrots, onion, garlic, yellow pepper, cayenne pepper, red lentils, broth, water, and salt.
2. Cook on LOW for 6 hours.
3. Add the lemon zest, juice, and rosemary. Season with salt and pepper.
4. Pour into bowls and garnish with extra chopped rosemary.

Nutrition facts per serving
Calories 410, total fat 25g, carbs 69 g, protein 29 g,
Sodium 680 mg, sugar 6 g

Lentil and Potato Soup

Warm, comforting lentil soup can be in your belly in couple of hours.

Serves 4 – Preparation time 20minutes – Cooking time 8 hours

Ingredients
½ tablespoon olive oil
½ large yellow onion, chopped
½ celery stalk, sliced
½ large carrot, sliced
1 clove garlic, minced
½ large bunch Swiss chard, leaves torn into bite-sized pieces and stems sliced
½ cup dried brown lentils, picked over and rinsed
2 medium potatoes, cut into 1-inch pieces
3 cups vegetable broth
½ tablespoon soy sauce or tamari
Salt and pepper to taste

Preparation
1. Heat the oil in a large pan over medium heat. Add the onion, celery, carrot, garlic, and chard stalks. Cover and cook until tender, about 8–10 minutes, stirring occasionally.
2. Put the cooked vegetable mixture, lentils, potatoes, broth, and soy sauce in a 4- to 6-quart slow cooker. Stir to combine, cover, and cook on LOW for 8 hours.
3. Just before the soup is ready, boil a large pot of water. Put the reserved chard leaves in the boiling water and simmer for about 5 minutes. Drain well and stir them into the soup. Season with salt and pepper.

Nutrition facts per serving
Calories 175.3 total fat 5.1g, carbs 27 g, protein 9.6 g,
Sodium 396.1 mg, sugar 3.6 g

Butternut Squash and Parsnip Soup

This delicious butternut squash and parsnip soup will warm you up on a cold winter's night. Serve with fresh bread and a salad for a complete meal.

Serves 4 – Preparation time 20 minutes – Cooking time 8 hours

Ingredients
2 ½ cups butternut squash, peeled, seeded, and chopped
1 cup parsnips, peeled and chopped
1 cup onion, chopped
½ cup apple, peeled and chopped
1 cup vegetable broth
½ teaspoon salt
¼ teaspoon black pepper
¼ teaspoon dried thyme
⅛ teaspoon paprika
¼ cup soy or almond milk

Preparation
1. Combine all the ingredients EXCEPT the milk in a slow cooker. Cook on LOW for 6 hours, or HIGH for 3–4 hours
2. Once the vegetables are soft, purée the soup in a blender in until smooth.
3. Return the soup to the slow cooker and stir in the milk.

Nutrition facts per serving
Calories 238 total fat 9.2 g, carbs 35.3 g, protein 6 g,
Sodium 199 mg, sugar 9.9 g

Desserts

Caramel Poached Peaches

This easy dessert is bursting with juicy apples, brown sugar, and an oat crumble topping.

Serves 4 – Preparation time 10 minutes – Cooking time 4 hours

Ingredients
For the peaches:
1 cup brown sugar
½ cup granulated sugar
5 large peaches, peeled and cut into chunks
¼ teaspoon salt
1 teaspoon cinnamon

For the topping:
⅔ cup oats
⅔ cup loosely packed brown sugar
¼ cup flour
½ teaspoon cinnamon
3–4 tablespoons soft margarine
1 teaspoon vanilla extract

Preparation
1. Mix the brown sugar, granulated sugar, apples, salt, and cinnamon in a mixing bowl. Layer the mixture on the bottom of the slow cooker.
2. Combine the oats, brown sugar, flour, cinnamon, margarine, and vanilla extract. Sprinkle the mixture over the apples. Cook on LOW for 4 hours.
3. Turn off the heat and let it sit for an hour, to thicken the caramel.

Nutrition facts per serving
Calories 275 total fat 3.4 g, carbs 82.7 g, protein 0 g,
Sodium 32.1 mg, sugar 76.5 g

Lemon Blueberry Cake

This blueberry lemon cake recipe is perfect for spring.

Serves 4 – Preparation time 10 minutes – Cooking time 1 hour

Ingredients
½ cup whole wheat pastry flour
¼ teaspoon stevia, or to taste
¼ teaspoon baking powder
⅓ cup unsweetened non-dairy milk
¼ cup blueberries
1 teaspoon ground flax seed mixed with 2 teaspoons warm water
1 teaspoon olive oil
½ teaspoon lemon zest
¼ teaspoon vanilla extract
¼ teaspoon lemon extract

Preparation
1. Spray the slow cooker with oil.
2. Combine the flour, stevia, and baking powder in a medium bowl.
3. In a separate bowl, mix the non-dairy milk, blueberries, flax seed with water, olive oil, lemon zest, vanilla extract, and lemon extract.
4. Add the wet ingredients to the dry, and mix until combined.
5. Pour the mixture into the slow cooker and spread it evenly on the bottom.
6. Put a clean dish towel or paper towel between the lid and slow cooker to absorb the condensation. Cook on HIGH for 1 hour, or until the middle is firm.

Nutrition facts per serving
Calories 182.5, total fat 2.3 g, carbs 37.4 g, protein 4.0 g,
Sodium 390 mg, sugar 15 g

Caramel Mocha Cheesecake

It is hard to believe that you can cook a cheesecake…a VEGAN CHEESECAKE in your crock pot, but you sure can.

Serves 4– Preparation time 10 minutes – Cooking time 4 hours

Ingredients

Mocha cheesecake:

¾ cup ground vegan chocolate graham crackers or chocolate wafers (such as chocolate chip Teddy Grahams®)

4 tablespoons margarine, melted

⅓ cup sugar

8 ounces vegan cream cheese, softened

1 banana

1 ounce bittersweet vegan chocolate, melted and slightly cooled

½ teaspoon pure vanilla extract

½ teaspoon instant coffee

⅛ teaspoon salt

Salted caramel:

4 tablespoons margarine

1 cup brown sugar, packed

½ cup almond milk

½ teaspoon sea salt or Kosher salt

1 tablespoon pure vanilla extract

Cashew cream for serving (optional)

Preparation

1. Coat six 4-ounce ramekins with a non-stick spray.
2. Mix the crushed grahams with the margarine and a pinch of salt. In each ramekin, put a tablespoon and a teaspoon of the crust mixture. Press the crust into a uniform layer.
3. Beat the sugar and vegan cream cheese in a large bowl until smooth. Add the banana and mix until combined. Mix in the melted chocolate, vanilla, instant coffee, and salt. Pour the filling into each ramekin up to ¾ of its capacity and place it in the slow cooker.
4. Carefully pour warm water around the ramekins until three-quarters is submerged. Cover and cook for 1 ½ hours on HIGH.
5. When the cheesecakes are set, carefully remove them from the slow cooker and refrigerate for 2 hours.
6. To make the salted caramel, combine the margarine, brown sugar, almond milk, and salt in a medium saucepan. Cook for 7 minutes over medium heat, stirring occasionally. Add the vanilla and cook for 1 more minute to thicken. Pour the caramel into a mason jar, and refrigerate until it is cold.
7. Spoon salted caramel sauce and cashew cream over each cheesecake just before serving.

Nutrition facts per serving

Calories 370, total fat 14 g, carbs 53 g, protein 10 g, Sodium 290 mg sugar 46.5 g

Triple Chocolate-Peanut Butter Pudding Cake

This delicious recipe for slow cooked cake will satisfy all cravings. Three kinds of chocolate give this slow-cooked cake its characteristic chocolate flavor.

Serves 4 – Preparation time 20 minutes – Cooking time 2 hours

Ingredients
Nonstick cooking spray
1 cup all-purpose flour
⅓ cup sugar
2 tablespoons unsweetened cocoa powder
1 ½ teaspoons baking powder
½ cup chocolate almond milk
2 tablespoons vegetable oil
2 teaspoons vanilla
½ cup vegan peanut butter-flavored baking chips
½ cup chocolate pieces
½ cup chopped peanuts
¾ cup sugar
2 tablespoons unsweetened cocoa powder
1 ½ cups boiling water
Vegan chocolate pieces (optional, to garnish)

Preparation
1. Lightly coat the inside of a 4-quart slow cooker with cooking spray, or line the bowl with parchment paper.
2. In a medium bowl, mix the flour, sugar, cocoa powder, and baking powder. Add the chocolate almond milk, oil, and vanilla. Stir just until moistened.

3. Stir in the peanut butter baking ships, the chocolate pieces, and peanuts.
4. Spread the mixture in the slow cooker.
5. In another medium bowl, mix ¾ cup sugar and 2 tablespoons cocoa powder. Slowly add the boiling water. Carefully pour the hot cocoa mixture onto the mixture in the slow cooker.
6. Cover, and cook on HIGH for 2–2 ½ hours, or until a toothpick inserted in the center of the cake comes out clean.
7. Remove the liner from the bowl, if possible, or turn off the pot. Let the cake rest for 30–40 minutes, to cool slightly.
8. To serve, spoon the cake onto serving dishes and garnish with chocolate pieces.

Nutrition facts per serving
Calories 276.5, total fat 13.7 g, carbs 29.3 g, protein 5.1 g, Sodium 357 mg, sugar 10.6 g

Apple Crisp

An easy way to make a wonderful, comforting meal with these abundantly falling apples!

Serves 6– Preparation time 30 minutes – Cooking time 3 hours

Ingredients
1 cup all-purpose flour
½ cup light brown sugar
½ cup white sugar
½ teaspoon ground cinnamon
¼ teaspoon ground nutmeg
1 pinch salt
½ cup margarine
1 cup chopped walnuts
⅓ cup white sugar, or to taste
1 tablespoon cornstarch
½ teaspoon ground ginger
½ teaspoon ground cinnamon
6 cups apples, peeled, cored, and chopped
2 tablespoons lemon juice

Preparation
1. Mix the flour, brown sugar, ½ cup white sugar, ½ teaspoon cinnamon, nutmeg, and salt in a bowl. Combine the margarine with the flour mixture, using your fingers or a fork, until coarse crumbs form. Stir in the nuts and set the bowl aside.
2. Whisk together ⅓ cup of sugar, cornstarch, ginger, and ½ teaspoon of cinnamon.
3. Put the apples in a slow cooker, and incorporate the cornstarch mixture. Mix in the lemon juice.

4. Sprinkle the crumble mixture on top. Cover and cook for 2 hours on HIGH, or 4 hours on LOW, until the apples are soft.
5. Let the dish cool for an hour before serving.

Nutrition facts per serving
Calories 187, total fat 7.7 g, carbs 30.2 g, protein 1.5 g, Sodium 147.6 mg, sugar 12 g

Turmeric Rice Pudding

Fragrant, rich, and deliciously creamy.

Serves 2 – Preparation time 10 minutes – Cooking time 6 hours

Ingredients
½ cup rice
1 ½ cups almond milk
1 teaspoon vanilla
½ teaspoon ground cinnamon
½ teaspoon turmeric powder
¼ teaspoon freshly grated ginger root
Pinch black pepper
1 tablespoon coconut oil
2 large pitted dates, minced

Preparation
1. Combine all the ingredients in the bowl of a slow cooker.
2. Cook on LOW for 6 hours, until the rice is soft and the milk is absorbed.
3. If is a little dry, you can add more almond milk.

Nutrition facts per serving
Calories 157, total fat 9.9g, carbs 15.5 g, protein 1.6 g, Sodium 0.8 mg, sugar 9.4 g

Berry Cobbler

This is a super simple dessert packed with strawberries and blueberries (fresh or frozen!) and is perfect for summer or winter.

Serves 4 – Preparation time 10 minutes – Cooking time 2 hours

Ingredients
Cobbler Batter
1 cup flour
2 tablespoons sugar
1 teaspoon baking powder
½ teaspoon ground cinnamon
2 bananas, mashed
½ cup coconut or almond milk
2 tablespoons canola oil

Berry Mixture
4 tablespoons flour
1 cup sugar
4 cups mixed berries of choice, fresh or frozen

Preparation
1. Make the batter. In a large bowl, mix the flour, sugar, baking powder, and cinnamon. Stir in the banana, milk, and oil until combined. The batter will be thick.
2. Lightly grease a 4- to 5-quart slow cooker and spread the batter in the bottom.
3. In another large bowl, mix the flour and sugar. Stir in the berries and spread them over the dough in a slow cooker.
4. Cover and cook on HIGH for 2–3 hours (closer to 2 hours for fresh or thawed berries, closer to 3 hours for frozen berries). Serve hot, with a splash of almond milk.

Nutrition facts per serving
Calories 253, total fat 9 g, carbs 42 g, protein 4 g,
Sodium 371 mg, sugar 12 g

Recipe Index

More Books by Sarah Spencer

Here are some of Sarah Spencer's other cookbooks.

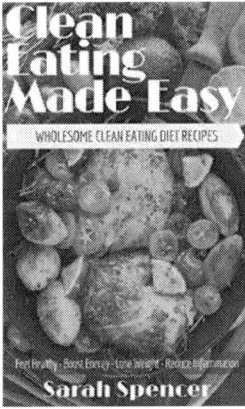

Clean Eating Made Easy
WHOLESOME CLEAN EATING DIET RECIPES
Feel Healthy - Boost Energy - Lose Weight - Reduce Inflammation
Sarah Spencer

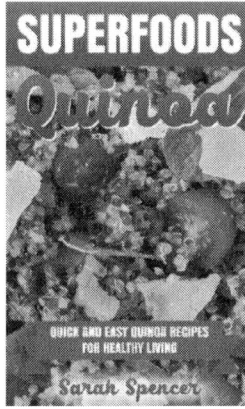

SUPERFOODS
Quinoa
QUICK AND EASY QUINOA RECIPES FOR HEALTHY LIVING
Sarah Spencer

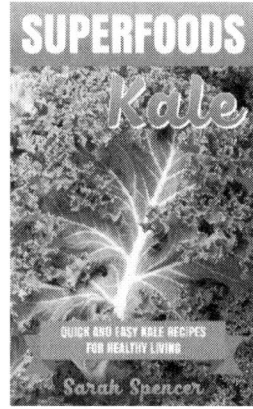

SUPERFOODS
Kale
QUICK AND EASY KALE RECIPES FOR HEALTHY LIVING
Sarah Spencer

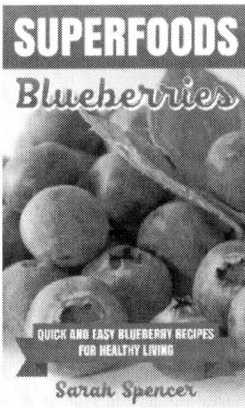

SUPERFOODS
Blueberries
QUICK AND EASY BLUEBERRY RECIPES FOR HEALTHY LIVING
Sarah Spencer

SUPERFOODS
Chia Seeds
QUICK AND EASY CHIA SEEDS RECIPES FOR HEALTHY LIVING
Sarah Spencer

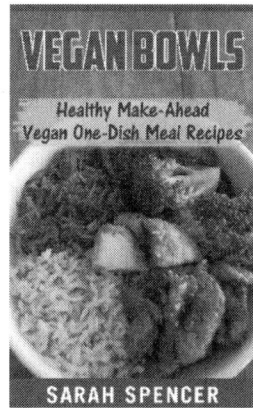

VEGAN BOWLS
Healthy Make-Ahead Vegan One-Dish Meal Recipes
SARAH SPENCER

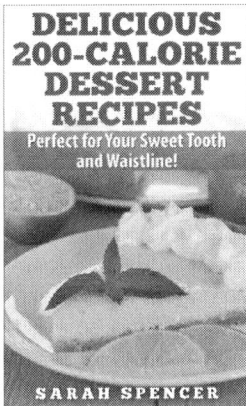

DELICIOUS 200-CALORIE DESSERT RECIPES
Perfect for Your Sweet Tooth and Waistline!
SARAH SPENCER

NO SUGAR ADDED
HEALTHY FROZEN DESSERT Recipes
Ice Pop, Slush, Sorbet, Treat on Stick, Frozen Yogurt, Frozen drink, Pie, Bar, Parfait and More
LOUISE DAVIDSON

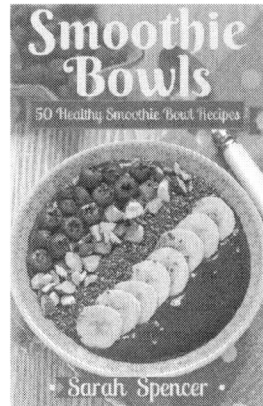

Smoothie Bowls
50 Healthy Smoothie Bowl Recipes
Sarah Spencer

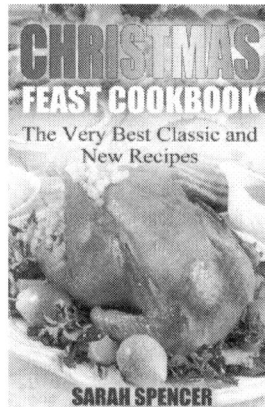

Appendix – Cooking Conversion Charts

1. Measuring Equivalent Chart

Type	Imperial	Imperial	Metric
Weight	1 dry ounce		28g
	1 pound	16 dry ounces	0.45 kg
Volume	1 teaspoon		5 ml
	1 dessert spoon	2 teaspoons	10 ml
	1 tablespoon	3 teaspoons	15 ml
	1 Australian tablespoon	4 teaspoons	20 ml
	1 fluid ounce	2 tablespoons	30 ml
	1 cup	16 tablespoons	240 ml
	1 cup	8 fluid ounces	240 ml
	1 pint	2 cups	470 ml
	1 quart	2 pints	0.95 l
	1 gallon	4 quarts	3.8 l
Length	1 inch		2.54 cm

* Numbers are rounded to the closest equivalent

2. Oven Temperature Equivalent Chart

Fahrenheit (°F)	Celsius (°C)	Gas Mark
220	100	
225	110	1/4
250	120	1/2
275	140	1
300	150	2
325	160	3
350	180	4
375	190	5
400	200	6
425	220	7
450	230	8
475	250	9
500	260	

* Celsius (°C) = T (°F)-32] * 5/9

** Fahrenheit (°F) = T (°C) * 9/5 + 32

*** Numbers are rounded to the closest equivalent

Printed in Poland
by Amazon Fulfillment
Poland Sp. z o.o., Wrocław